THE LITTLE ARCHITECT'S

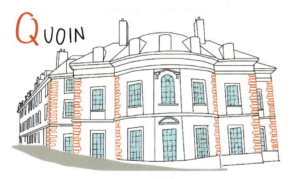
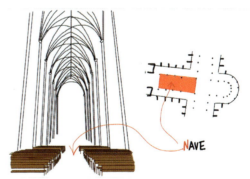

ALPHABET
LEARNING YOUR LETTERS THROUGH DESIGN.

Lora Nicole Teagarden, AIA, LEED AP BD+C©

Copyright © 2020 Lora Nicole Teagarden
All rights reserved.
ISBN-13: 978-1717112750

To James,

You are the kindest and smartest little bear I know. Go build your dreams. I can't wait to see what you create.

Love, Auntie LT

A is for Architecture
and buildings big & small.

A IS ALSO FOR...

Arch
A CURVED OBJECT THAT IS SUPPORTED AT BOTH ENDS

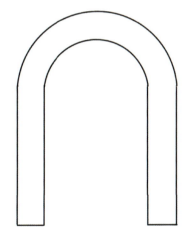

Archway
AN ARCH WITH VERTICAL SUPPORTS THAT YOU CAN PASS UNDER

Arcade
A SERIES OF ARCHWAYS THAT CREATE A LARGER OPENING

BRICK TYPES

 SOLID STANDARD

 CORED STANDARD

 KING

 MODULAR

 UTILITY

 NORMAN

 8-SQUARE

PATTERNS

 RUNNING

 COMMON

 ENGLISH

 STACK

 DUTCH

 FLEMISH

USES

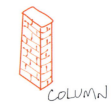 WALL

COLUMN

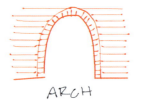 ARCH

B IS FOR Bricks OF ALL SHAPES AND SIZES.

B is also for...

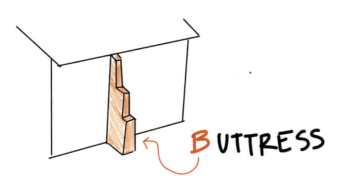

Buttress

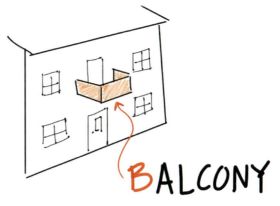

Balcony

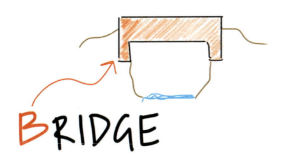

Bridge

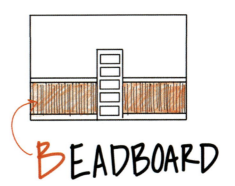

Beadboard

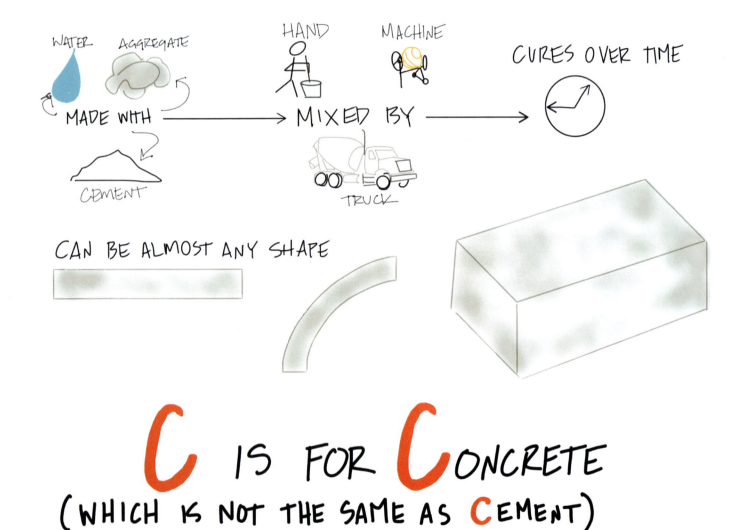

C IS ALSO FOR...

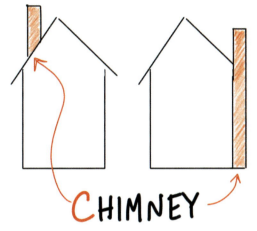

CHIMNEY

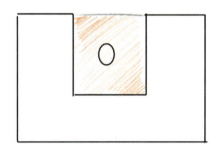

COURTYARD

COLUMN

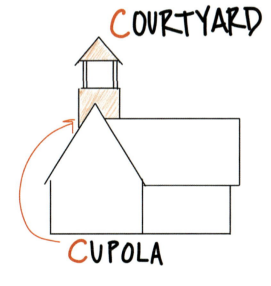

CUPOLA

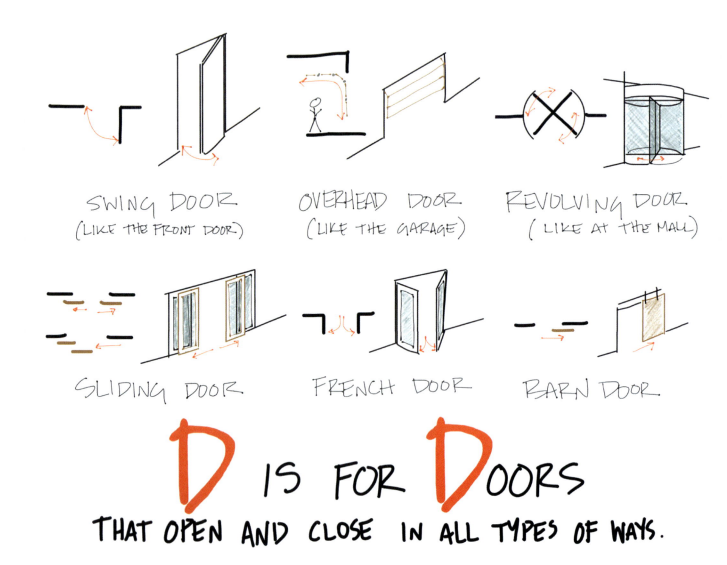

D IS ALSO FOR...

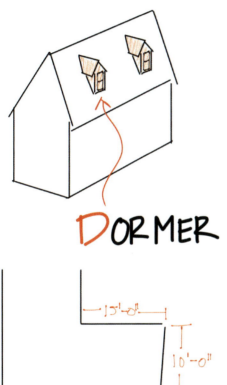
DORMER

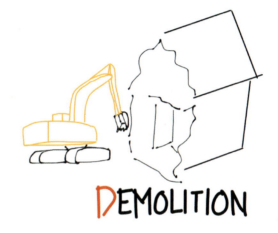
DEMOLITION

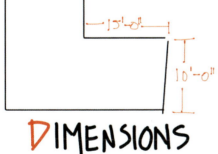
DIMENSIONS

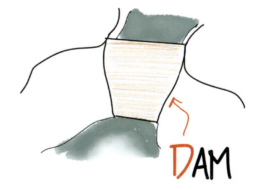
DAM

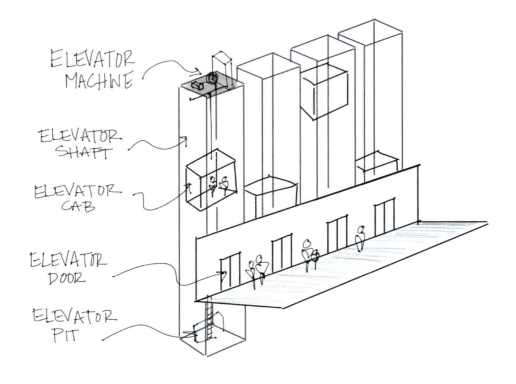

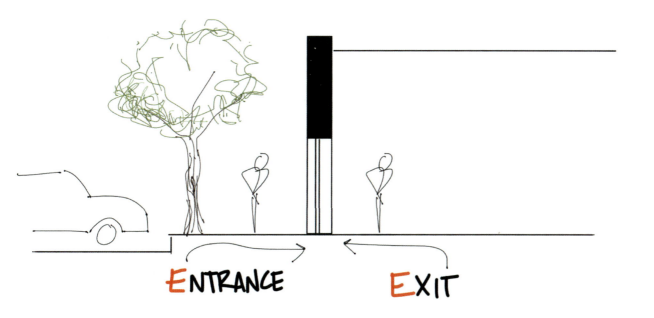

F IS FOR Foundation
WHICH HOLDS A BUILDING STRONG AND STEADY.

CIRCLE — NO SIDES

SQUARE — 4 SIDES

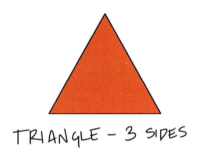
TRIANGLE — 3 SIDES

PENTAGON — 5 SIDES

G IS FOR GEOMETRY —
THERE ARE SHAPES ALL AROUND US!

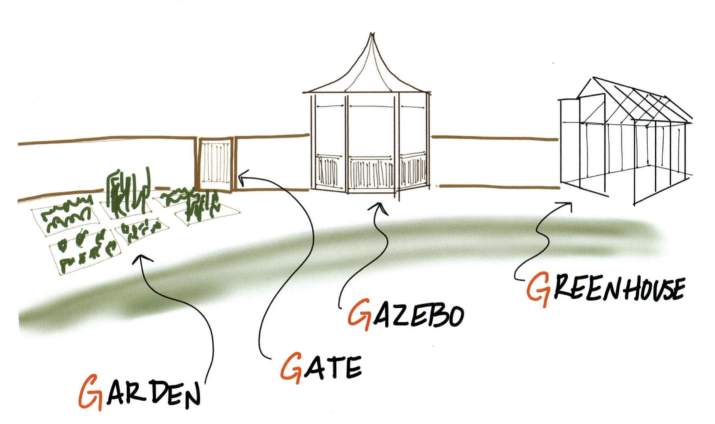

H is for Home.
They come in all shapes and sizes.

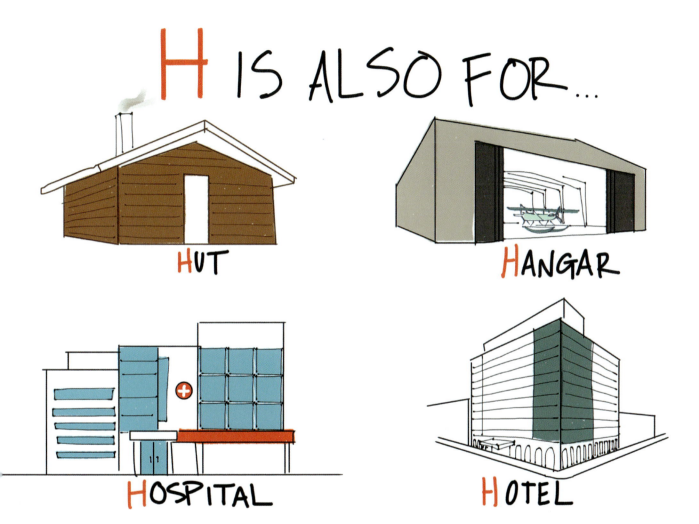

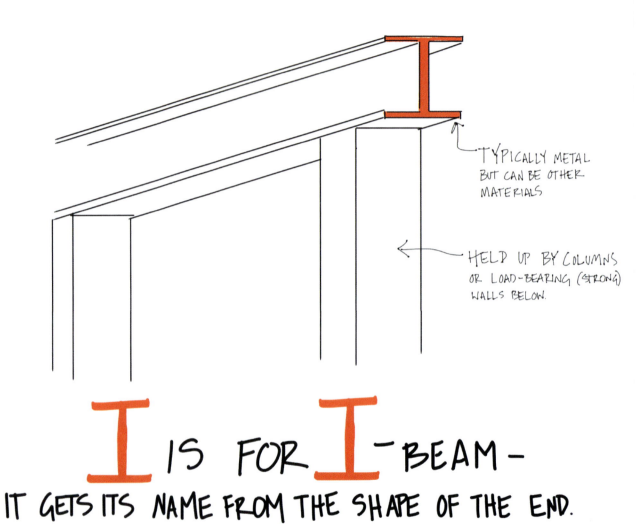

I IS ALSO FOR...

I GLOO

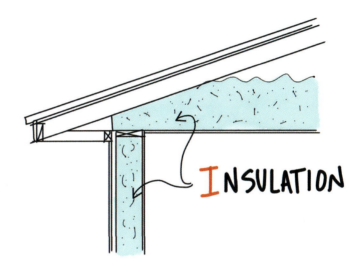

I NSULATION

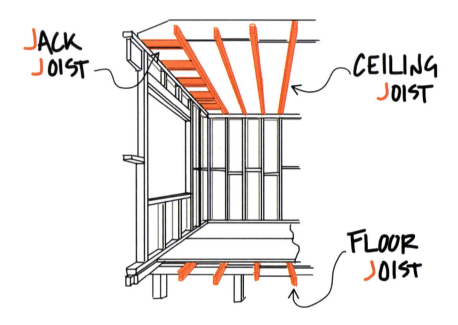

J IS ALSO FOR...

 BUTT JOINT

 MITER JOINT

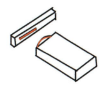 BISCUIT JOINT

 HALF-LAP JOINT

 BOX JOINT

 RABBET JOINT

 DADO JOINT

 TONGUE AND GROOVE JOINT

 MORTISE AND TENON JOINT

JOINERY

K is also for...

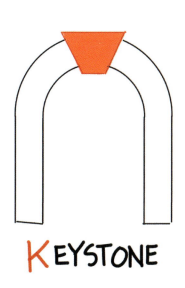

Keystone

Tower Keep
(this one is in London!)

SEATTLE PUBLIC LIBRARY

L IS FOR LIBRARY
WHERE YOU LISTEN, LEARN, AND LOOK!

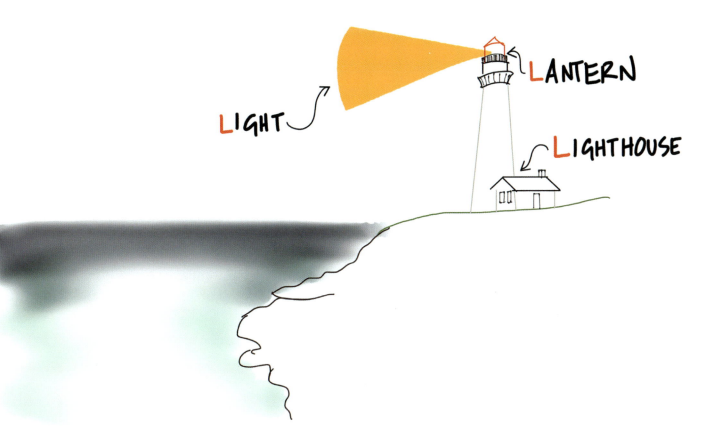

M IS FOR MAILBOX
WHERE YOU GET CARDS AND BOOKS!

M is also for...

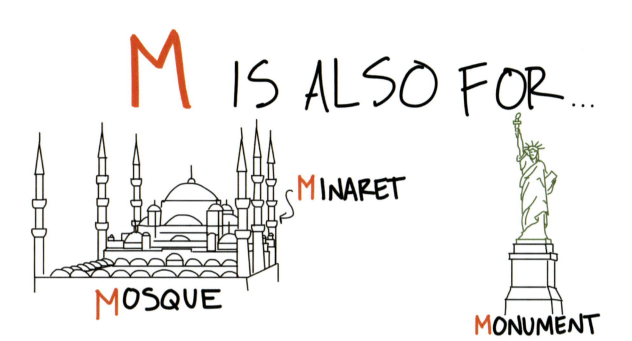

MINARET

MOSQUE

MONUMENT

MOBILE HOME

MUSEUM

O IS ALSO FOR...

OFFICE

OBSERVATORY

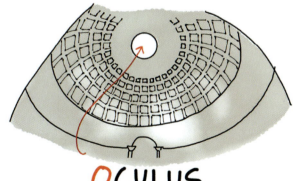

OCULUS

OBELISK

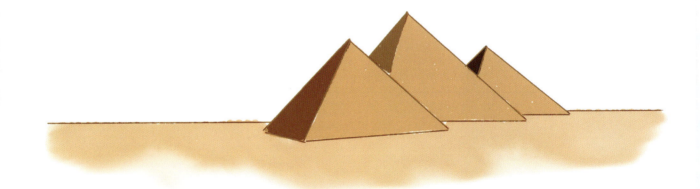

P IS FOR PYRAMID
THEY ARE TRIANGLES STANDING UP. CAN YOU SEE THEM?

P IS ALSO FOR...

PAGODA

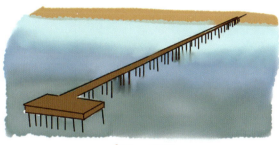
PIER

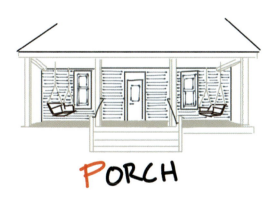
PORCH

PARK

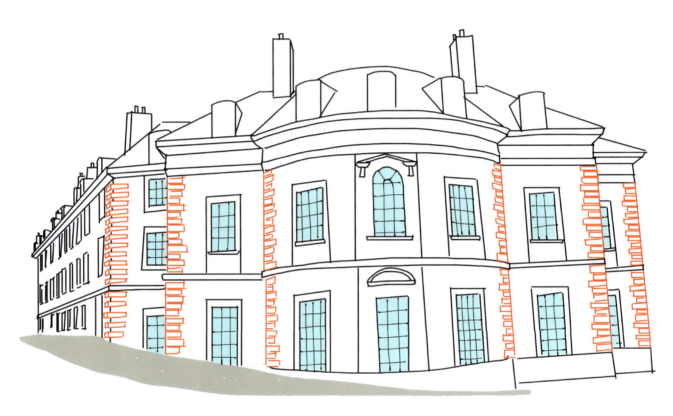

Q IS FOR QUOIN –
THEY ARE SPECIAL BLOCKS ON BUILDING CORNERS.

Q IS ALSO FOR...

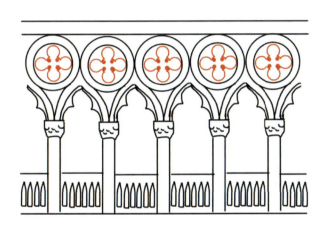

QUATREFOIL

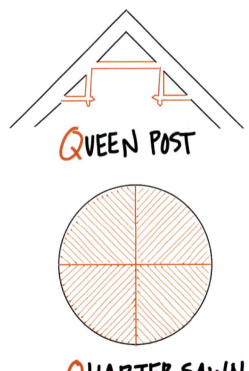

QUEEN POST

QUARTER SAWN

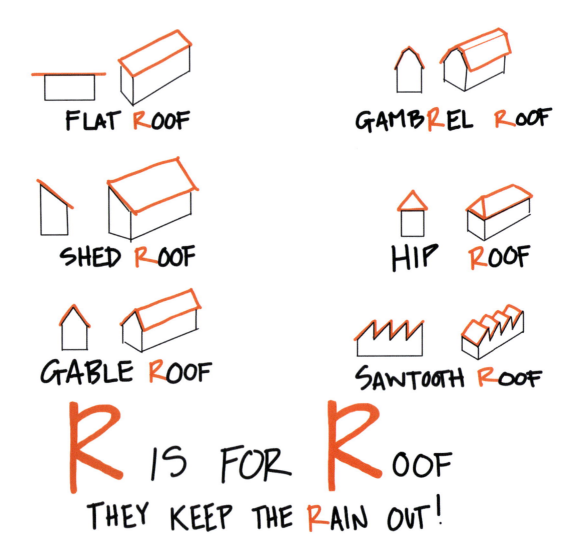

R IS ALSO FOR...

RAILING

RADIATOR

ROOM

RUG

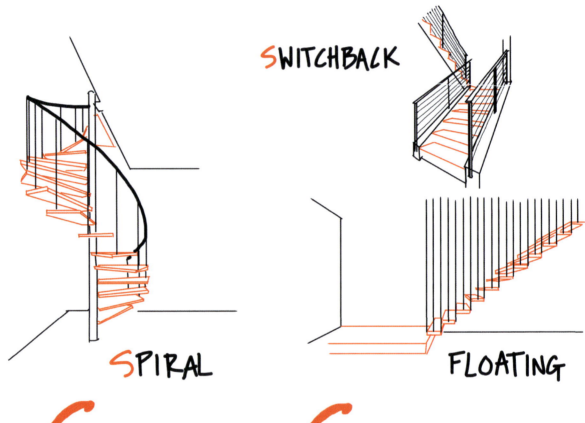

S IS ALSO FOR...

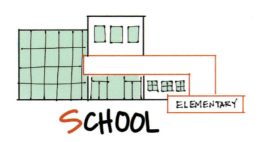
SCHOOL

SKYSCRAPER

STORE

STADIUM

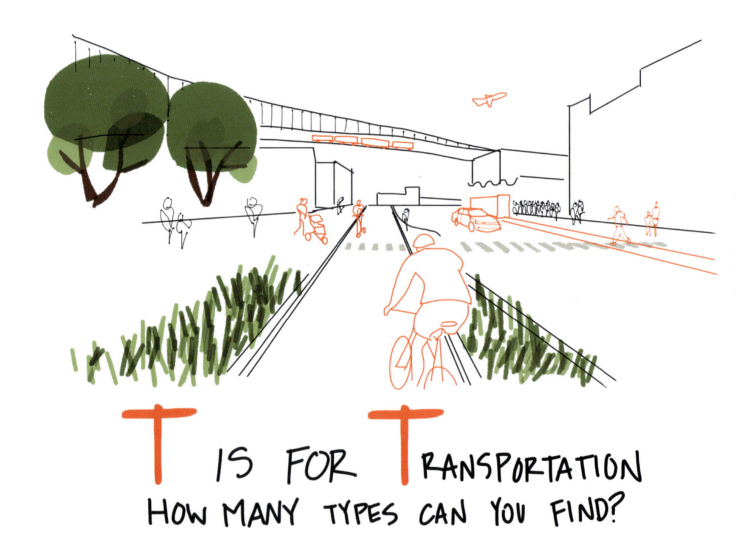

T IS ALSO FOR...

Teepee

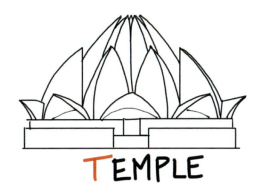
Temple

THIS ONE LEANS!
Tower

Tunnel

U IS FOR University —
WHERE YOU CONTINUE TO LEARN AND GROW.

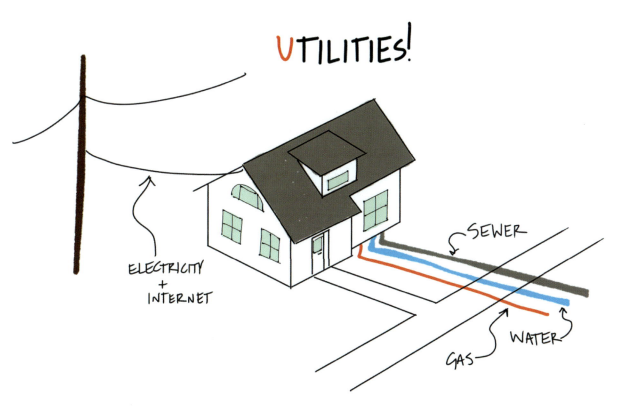

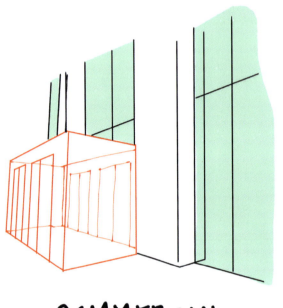

COMMERCIAL   RESIDENTIAL

V IS FOR Vestibule —
IT SEPARATES OUTSIDE FROM INSIDE.

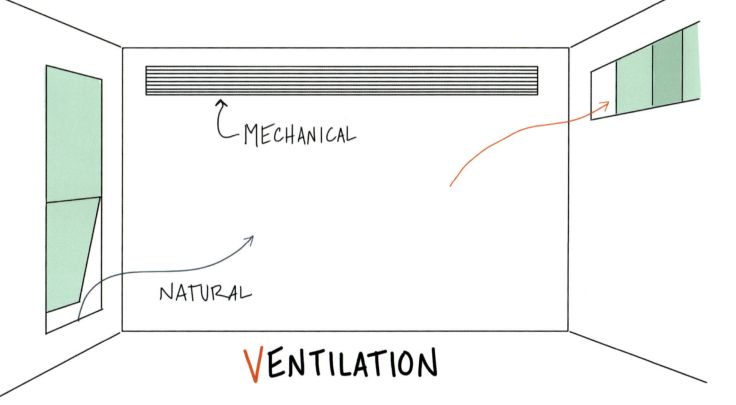

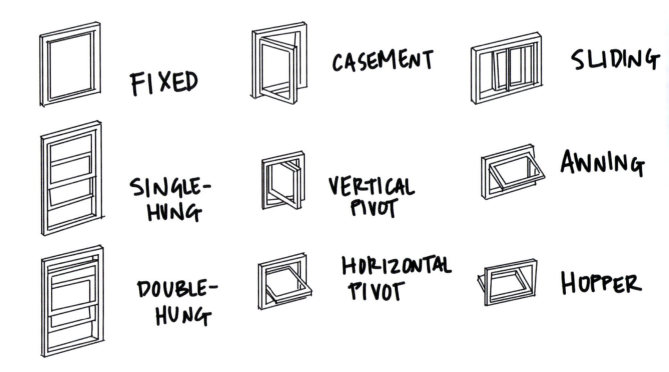

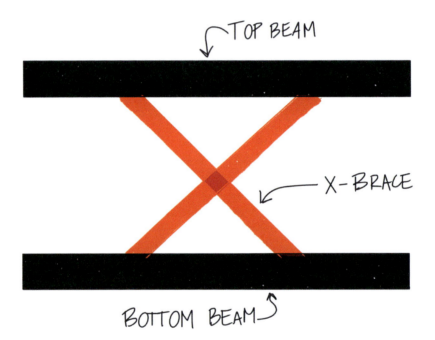

X IS FOR X-BRACE
IT HOLDS UP BUILDINGS, WALLS, BRIDGES, AND MORE

Y is for Yurt—
it's a round home made of canvas!

Y CAN BE USED IN BUILDING SHAPES, TOO!

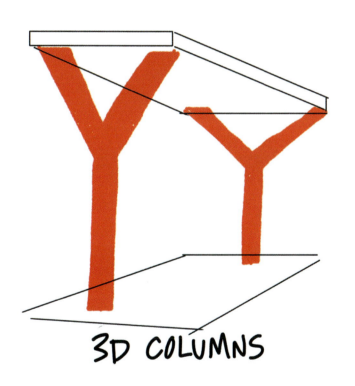

3D COLUMNS

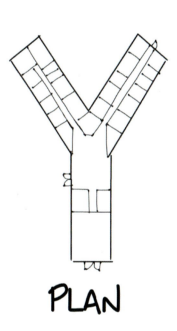

PLAN

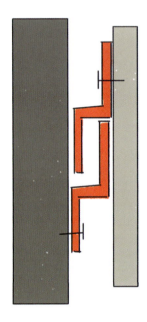

Z IS FOR Z-CLIP
THEY HELP CONNECT BUILDING MATERIALS.

CAN YOU FIND THE Z IN EACH IMAGE?

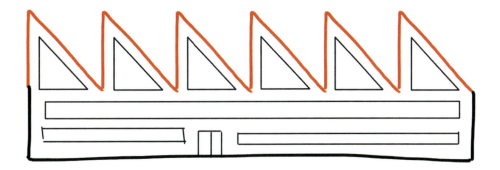

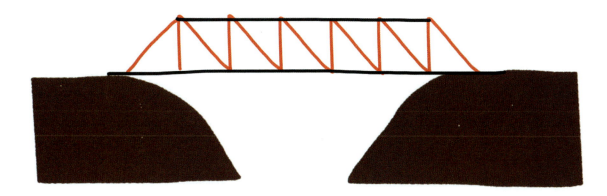

Printed by Amazon Italia Logistica S.r.l.
Torrazza Piemonte (TO), Italy